D1109563

Picture Acknowledgments

Ann Ronan Picture Library: pp. 7 (*The Shipwreck*, Joseph Mallord William Turner [1775–1851]), 8 (*Wheatfield with Crows*, Vincent Van Gogh [1853–90]), 11 (*Christ on the Sea of Galilee*, Jacopo Tintoretto [1518–94]), 21 (*Jesus Raising Lazarus*, after *Armenian Evangelistery* [c. 1269], Toros Rosline), 23 (*The Lady Musicians*, anonymous [16th century]), 26 (*King David Playing a 'Lyre'*, 10th–11th-century manuscript of St Martial de Limoges), 31 (*Monk Succouring a Pilgrim*, Claude Bonnefond [1796–1860]), 37 (*The Boulevard in Brussels*, Franz Gailliard [1861–1932]), 44 (*The Porter*, Francisco de Goya [1746–1828]), 46 (*Carrying the Cross*, Hieronymus Bosch [1460–1516]), 48 (Kariye Museum: *Jesus and the Saints* from the cupola, Church of Christ in Chora), 56–57 (*Yacht Approaching the Coast*, Joseph Mallord William Turner [1775–1851]), 59 (*Fire in a Town*, Daniel Van Heil [1604–62]), 69 (*St Rita de Cascia*, anonymous [19th century]), 77 (*St Mark the Evangelist*, Valentin de Boulogne [1591–1632]), 79 (*Dead-Wood Gatherer*, Mihaly Munkacsy [1844–1900]), 85 (*The Disciples Peter and John Running to the Sepulchre on the Morning of the Resurrection*, E. Burnard [1850–1921]), 91 (*The Angel Appearing to the Shepherds*, Pieter Bout [1658–1719]), 94 (*Elysium: Fragment of Last Judgement*, after Fra Angelico [1387–1455]).

Edimedia Collection: pp. 16 (*Spring*, Isaac Levitan [1860–1900]), 18 (*Summit Lake Near Lenchoile*, Fraser John Arthur [1838–98]), 29 (*Seaside at Palavas*, Gustave Courbet [1819–77]), 33 (*Old Man in Sorrow* [*On the Threshold of Eternity*], Vincent Van Gogh [1853–90]), 39 (*Water Lilies in the Morning*, Claude Monet [1840–1926]), 51 (*Path Leading to the High Grass*, Auguste Renoir [1841–1919]), 61 (*Young Girl Reading a Letter*, Peter Ilsted [1861–1933]), 63 (*Prisoners Exercising*, Vincent Van Gogh [1853–90]), 66 (*The Days Have Returned* [1871], Alexei Savlassov), 70 (*The Third Temptation*, William Blake [1757–1827]), 73 (*Reflections in a Stream*, Carl Julian Lund [1857–1936]), 82 (*Woody Landscape*, Carl Julian Lund [1857–1936]), 89 (*English Bestiary* [12th century]).

Heritage Images: pp. 25 (British Museum: *A Cornfield by Moonlight with the Evening Star*, Samuel Palmer [1805–81]), 35 (Corporation of London: *Ribbed and Paled in by Rocks Unscaleable*, Peter Graham [1836–1921]), 53 (British Library: *Creation* [c. 1340–c. 1370], from *La Bible Hystoriaux en Français*), 75 (British Library: *St John and the Angel* [c. 1310–c. 1325]).

Photos12.com: pp. 13 (ARJ: *The Wave*, Ivan Ayvazovsky [1817–1900]), 42 (Roman fresco representing the weighing of Good and Evil), 55 (ARJ: *Concert of Angels*, Philippe de Champaigne [1602–74]), 87 (ARJ: *Starry Night Over the Rhone*, Vincent Van Gogh [1853–90]).

To my godparents Lore and Hugh,
and to Rosalind and Ania

LOYOLAPRESS.

3441 N. ASHLAND AVENUE
CHICAGO, ILLINOIS 60657
(800) 621-1008
WWW.LOYOLABOOKS.ORG

First published in North America in 2004 by Loyola Press.
ISBN 0-8294-2058-4

Text copyright © 2003 Martin H. Manser. Original edition
published in English under the title *A Treasury of Psalms*
by Lion Publishing plc, Oxford, England.

Copyright © Lion Publishing plc 2003

The author asserts the moral right
to be identified as the author of this work

All rights reserved

Acknowledgments
Scripture quotations taken from the *Holy Bible, New
International Version*, copyright © 1973, 1978, 1984
International Bible Society. Used by permission of
Zondervan and Hodder & Stoughton Limited. All rights
reserved. The 'NIV' and 'New International Version'
trademarks are registered in the United States Patent and
Trademark Office by International Bible Society. Use of
either trademark requires the permission of International
Bible Society. UK trademark number 1448790.

Scripture quotations contained herein from The New
Revised Standard Version of the Bible, Anglicized Edition,
are copyright © 1989, 1995 by the Division of Christian
Education of the National Council of the Churches of
Christ in the United States of America, and are used by
permission. All rights reserved.

Extracts from the Authorized Version of the Bible (The
King James Bible), the rights in which are vested in the
Crown, are reproduced by permission of the Crown's
Patentee, Cambridge University Press.

A catalogue record for this book is available
from the British Library

Typeset in 12/13 Venetian 301

Printed and bound in Singapore

04 05 06 07 08 09 10 10 9 8 7 6 5 4 3 2 1

Contents

Introduction

The phone rang. It was my twin sister, phoning from over 10,000 miles away. 'Are you sitting down?... Mother's died...' Completely unexpectedly, our mother, an active 77-year-old, had had a series of heart attacks, the last one proving fatal. As a family, we were shattered; we quickly came to the end of our human resources.

In the days immediately following my mother's death, and on many other occasions, the Psalms have taken on a deeper dimension for me. When I have no words of my own, I have found that I can pray the psalmist's words. The psalmist's honesty and realism usher us into God's presence. We are able to see our own lives and circumstances in the wider setting of God's perspective. We can see what God is like; we can make the Psalms our own and talk freely to him about the whole range of emotions that we experience: from fear and grief to joy and inspiration; from anger and despair to exuberant praise and adoration.

It is my hope and prayer that as you read the extracts in this *Treasury of Psalms*, you will be able to derive comfort, light and fresh courage for your life's journey.

Martin H. Manser

When You Are
Afraid

The LORD is my light and my salvation;
  whom shall I fear?
The LORD is the stronghold of my life;
  of whom shall I be afraid?

When evildoers assail me
  to devour my flesh —

my adversaries and foes —
  they shall stumble and fall.

Though an army encamp against me,
  my heart shall not fear;
though war rise up against me,
  yet I will be confident.

One thing I asked of the LORD,
  that will I seek after:
to live in the house of the LORD
  all the days of my life,
to behold the beauty of the LORD,
  and to inquire in his temple.

For he will hide me in his shelter
  in the day of trouble;
he will conceal me under the cover
    of his tent;
  he will set me high on a rock.

Now my head is lifted up
  above my enemies all around me,
and I will offer in his tent
  sacrifices with shouts of joy;
I will sing and make melody to the LORD.

Hear, O LORD, when I cry aloud,
  be gracious to me and answer me!
'Come,' my heart says, 'seek his face!'
  Your face, LORD, do I seek.
  Do not hide your face from me.

Do not turn your servant away in anger,
  you who have been my help.
Do not cast me off, do not forsake me,
  O God of my salvation!
If my father and mother forsake me,
  the LORD will take me up.

Teach me your way, O LORD,
  and lead me on a level path
  because of my enemies.
Do not give me up to the will of my adversaries,
  for false witnesses have risen against me,
  and they are breathing out violence.

I believe that I shall see the goodness of the LORD
  in the land of the living.
Wait for the LORD;
  be strong, and let your heart take courage;
  wait for the LORD!

  Psalm 27

I sought the LORD, and he answered me,
  and delivered me from all my fears.
Look to him, and be radiant;
  so your faces shall never be ashamed.
This poor soul cried, and was heard by
      the LORD,
  and was saved from every trouble.
The angel of the LORD encamps
  around those who fear him, and delivers them.

  Psalm 34:4–7

God is our refuge and strength,
  an ever-present help in trouble.
Therefore we will not fear, though the earth give way
  and the mountains fall into the heart of the sea,
though its waters roar and foam
  and the mountains quake with their surging…

'Be still, and know that I am God;
  I will be exalted among the nations,
  I will be exalted in the earth.'

The LORD Almighty is with us;
  the God of Jacob is our fortress.

  Psalm 46:1–3, 10–11

My heart is in anguish within me,
  the terrors of death have fallen upon me.
Fear and trembling come upon me,
  and horror overwhelms me.
And I say, 'O that I had wings like a dove!
  I would fly away and be at rest;
truly, I would flee far away;
  I would lodge in the wilderness;
I would hurry to find a shelter for myself
  from the raging wind and tempest.'…

Cast your burden on the LORD,
  and he will sustain you;
he will never permit
  the righteous to be moved.

Psalm 55:4–8, 22

He who dwells in the shelter of the Most High
  will rest in the shadow of the Almighty.
I will say of the LORD, 'He is my refuge and my fortress,
  my God, in whom I trust.'

Surely he will save you from the fowler's snare
  and from the deadly pestilence.
He will cover you with his feathers,
  and under his wings you will find refuge;
  his faithfulness will be your shield and rampart.
You will not fear the terror of night,
  nor the arrow that flies by day,
nor the pestilence that stalks in the darkness,
  nor the plague that destroys at midday…

If you make the Most High your dwelling –
  even the LORD, who is my refuge –
then no harm will befall you,
  no disaster will come near your tent.
For he will command his angels concerning you
  to guard you in all your ways;
they will lift you up in their hands,
  so that you will not strike your foot against a stone.
You will tread upon the lion and the cobra;
  you will trample the great lion and the serpent.

'Because he loves me,' says the LORD, 'I will
    rescue him;
  I will protect him, for he acknowledges my name.
He will call upon me, and I will answer him;

I will be with him in trouble,
   I will deliver him and honour him.
With long life will I satisfy him
   and show him my salvation.'

    Psalm 91:1–6, 9–16

O give thanks unto the LORD; for he is good:
   because his mercy endureth for ever.
Let Israel now say,
   that his mercy endureth for ever.
Let the house of Aaron now say,
   that his mercy endureth for ever.
Let them now that fear the LORD say,
   that his mercy endureth for ever.
I called upon the LORD in distress:
   the LORD answered me, and set me in a large place.
The LORD is on my side; I will not fear:
   what can man do unto me?
The LORD taketh my part with them that help me:
   therefore shall I see my desire upon them that
     hate me.
It is better to trust in the LORD
   than to put confidence in man.
It is better to trust in the LORD
   than to put confidence in princes…

The LORD is my strength and song,
   and is become my salvation.
The voice of rejoicing and salvation
   is in the tabernacles of the righteous:
   the right hand of the LORD doeth valiantly.

The right hand of the LORD is exalted:
   the right hand of the LORD doeth valiantly.
I shall not die, but live,
   and declare the works of the LORD.
The LORD hath chastened me sore:
   but he hath not given me over unto death.
Open to me the gates of righteousness:
   I will go into them, and I will praise the LORD:
This gate of the LORD,
   into which the righteous shall enter.
I will praise thee: for thou hast heard me,
   and art become my salvation.
The stone which the builders refused
   is become the head stone of the corner.
This is the LORD's doing;
   it is marvellous in our eyes.
This is the day which the LORD hath made;
   we will rejoice and be glad in it...

Thou art my God, and I will praise thee:
   thou art my God, I will exalt thee.
O give thanks unto the LORD; for he is good:
   for his mercy endureth for ever.

   Psalm 118:1–9, 14–24, 28–29

When You Are
Bereaved

The LORD is my shepherd; I shall not want.
He maketh me to lie down in green pastures:
  he leadeth me beside the still waters.
He restoreth my soul:
  he leadeth me in the paths of righteousness
  for his name's sake.
Yea, though I walk through the valley of the shadow
    of death,
  I will fear no evil:
for thou art with me;
  thy rod and thy staff
  they comfort me.
Thou preparest a table before me
  in the presence of mine enemies:
thou anointest my head with oil;
  my cup runneth over.
Surely goodness and mercy shall follow me
  all the days of my life:
and I will dwell in the house of the LORD
  for ever.

Psalm 23

In you, O LORD, I have taken refuge;
  let me never be put to shame.
Rescue me and deliver me in your
    righteousness;
  turn your ear to me and save me.
Be my rock of refuge,
  to which I can always go;
give the command to save me,
  for you are my rock and my fortress...

For you have been my hope, O Sovereign LORD,
  my confidence since my youth.
From my birth I have relied on you;
  you brought me forth from my mother's womb.
  I will ever praise you...

Be not far from me, O God;
  come quickly, O my God, to help me...

But as for me, I shall always have hope;
   I will praise you more and more.
My mouth will tell of your righteousness,
   of your salvation all day long,
      though I know not its measure.
I will come and proclaim your mighty acts,
      O Sovereign LORD;
   I will proclaim your righteousness, yours alone.
Since my youth, O God, you have taught me,
   and to this day I declare your marvellous deeds.
Even when I am old and grey,
   do not forsake me, O God,
till I declare your power to the next generation,
   your might to all who are to come.

Your righteousness reaches to the skies, O God,
   you who have done great things.
   Who, O God, is like you?
Though you have made me see troubles, many and
      bitter,
   you will restore my life again;
from the depths of the earth
   you will again bring me up.
You will increase my honour
   and comfort me once again.

   Psalm 71:1–3, 5–6, 12, 14–21

Whom have I in heaven but you?
   And there is nothing on earth that I desire other
      than you.
My flesh and my heart may fail,

but God is the strength of my heart and my
    portion for ever.

Indeed, those who are far from you will perish;
    you put an end to those who are false to you.
But for me it is good to be near God;
    I have made the Lord GOD my refuge,
    to tell of all your works.

      Psalm 73:25–28

I love the LORD, for he heard my voice;
    he heard my cry for mercy.
Because he turned his ear to me,
    I will call on him as long as I live.

The cords of death entangled me,
    the anguish of the grave came upon me;
    I was overcome by trouble and sorrow.
Then I called on the name of the LORD:
    'O LORD, save me!'

The LORD is gracious and righteous;
    our God is full of compassion.
The LORD protects the simple-hearted;
    when I was in great need, he saved me.

Be at rest once more, O my soul,
    for the LORD has been good to you.

For you, O LORD, have delivered my soul from death,
    my eyes from tears,

my feet from stumbling,
that I may walk before the LORD
  in the land of the living.
I believed; therefore I said,
  'I am greatly afflicted.'
And in my dismay I said,
  'All men are liars.'

How can I repay the LORD
  for all his goodness to me?
I will lift up the cup of salvation
  and call on the name of the LORD.
I will fulfil my vows to the LORD
  in the presence of all his people.

Precious in the sight of the LORD
  is the death of his saints.
O LORD, truly I am your servant;
  I am your servant, the son of your maidservant;
  you have freed me from my chains.

I will sacrifice a thank-offering to you
  and call on the name of the LORD.
I will fulfil my vows to the LORD
  in the presence of all his people,
in the courts of the house of the LORD —
  in your midst, O Jerusalem.

Praise the LORD.

Psalm 116

When You Are
Thankful

I will give thanks to the LORD with my whole heart;
  I will tell of all your wonderful deeds.
I will be glad and exult in you;
  I will sing praise to your name, O Most High.

When my enemies turned back,
  they stumbled and perished before you.
For you have maintained my just cause;
  you have sat on the throne giving righteous
    judgment…

The LORD is a stronghold for the oppressed,
  a stronghold in times of trouble.
And those who know your name put their trust
    in you,
  for you, O LORD, have not forsaken those who
    seek you.

Sing praises to the LORD, who dwells in Zion.
  Declare his deeds among the peoples.

  Psalm 9:1–4, 9–11

I will bless the LORD at all times:
  his praise shall continually be in my mouth.
My soul shall make her boast in the LORD:
  the humble shall hear thereof, and be glad.
O magnify the LORD with me,
  and let us exalt his name together.
I sought the LORD, and he heard me,
  and delivered me from all my fears.
They looked unto him, and were lightened:

and their faces were not ashamed.
This poor man cried, and the LORD heard him,
  and saved him out of all his troubles.
The angel of the LORD encampeth round about them
    that fear him,
  and delivereth them.
O taste and see that the LORD is good:
  blessed is the man that trusteth in him.
O fear the LORD, ye his saints:
  for there is no want to them that fear him.
The young lions do lack, and suffer hunger:
  but they that seek the LORD shall not want any
    good thing.

Psalm 34:1–10

It is a good thing to give
thanks unto the LORD,
and to sing praises unto
thy name, O most High:
To shew forth thy
lovingkindness in the
morning,
and thy faithfulness every
night,
Upon an instrument of ten
strings, and upon the
psaltery;
upon the harp with a
solemn sound.
For thou, LORD, hast made
me glad through thy
work:
I will triumph in the
works of thy hands.
O LORD, how great are thy
works!
and thy thoughts are very
deep.
A brutish man knoweth not;
neither doth a fool
understand this.
When the wicked spring as
the grass,
and when all the workers
of iniquity do flourish;
it is that they shall be
destroyed for ever:

But thou, LORD, art most high for evermore.
For, lo, thine enemies, O LORD,
  for, lo, thine enemies shall perish;
  all the workers of iniquity shall be scattered.
But my horn shalt thou exalt like the horn of an
    unicorn:
  I shall be anointed with fresh oil.
Mine eye also shall see my desire on mine enemies,
  and mine ears shall hear my desire of the wicked
    that rise up against me.
The righteous shall flourish like the palm tree:
  he shall grow like a cedar in Lebanon.
Those that be planted in the house of the LORD
  shall flourish in the courts of our God.
They shall still bring forth fruit in old age;
  they shall be fat and flourishing;
To shew that the LORD is upright:
  he is my rock, and there is no unrighteousness
    in him.

Psalm 92

O give thanks unto the LORD; for he is good:
  for his mercy endureth for ever.
O give thanks unto the God of gods:
  for his mercy endureth for ever.
O give thanks to the Lord of lords:
  for his mercy endureth for ever.
To him who alone doeth great wonders:
  for his mercy endureth for ever.
To him that by wisdom made the heavens:
  for his mercy endureth for ever.

To him that stretched out the earth above the waters:
   for his mercy endureth for ever.
To him that made great lights:
   for his mercy endureth for ever:
The sun to rule by day:
   for his mercy endureth for ever:
The moon and stars to rule by night:
   for his mercy endureth for ever.
To him that smote Egypt in their firstborn:
   for his mercy endureth for ever:
And brought out Israel from among them:
   for his mercy endureth for ever:
With a strong hand, and with a stretched out arm:
   for his mercy endureth for ever.
To him which divided the Red sea into parts:
   for his mercy endureth for ever:
And made Israel to pass through the midst of it:
   for his mercy endureth for ever...

Who remembered us in our low estate:
   for his mercy endureth for ever:
And hath redeemed us from our enemies:
   for his mercy endureth for ever.
Who giveth food to all flesh:
   for his mercy endureth for ever.
O give thanks unto the God of heaven:
   for his mercy endureth for ever.

Psalm 136:1–14, 23–26

I give you thanks, O LORD, with my whole heart;
   before the gods I sing your praise;

I bow down towards your holy temple
   and give thanks to your name for your steadfast
      love and your faithfulness;
   for you have exalted your name and your word
   above everything.
On the day I called, you answered me,
   you increased my strength of soul.

All the kings of the earth shall praise you, O LORD,
   for they have heard the words of your mouth.
They shall sing of the ways of the LORD,

for great is the glory of the LORD.
For though the LORD is high, he regards the lowly;
    but the haughty he perceives from far away.

Though I walk in the midst of trouble,
    you preserve me against the wrath of my enemies;
you stretch out your hand,
    and your right hand delivers me.
The LORD will fulfil his purpose for me;
    your steadfast love, O LORD, endures for ever.
    Do not forsake the work of your hands.

Psalm 138

When You Are
Ill or Weak

Be merciful to me, LORD, for I am faint;
 O LORD, heal me, for my bones are in agony.
My soul is in anguish.
 How long, O LORD, how long?

Turn, O LORD, and deliver me;
 save me because of your unfailing love…

I am worn out from groaning;
 all night long I flood my bed with weeping
 and drench my couch with tears.
My eyes grow weak with sorrow;
 they fail because of all my foes…

The LORD has heard my cry for mercy;
 the LORD accepts my prayer.

> Psalm 6:2–4, 6–7, 9

How long, O LORD? Will you forget me for ever?
 How long will you hide your face from me?
How long must I bear pain in my soul,
 and have sorrow in my heart all day long?
How long shall my enemy be exalted over me?

Consider and answer me, O LORD my God!
 Give light to my eyes, or I will sleep the sleep of
 death…

But I trusted in your steadfast love;
 my heart shall rejoice in your salvation.

> Psalm 13:1–3, 5

Unto thee will I cry, O LORD my rock;
  be not silent to me:
lest, if thou be silent to me,
  I become like them that go down into the pit.
Hear the voice of my supplications,
  when I cry unto thee,
when I lift up my hands
  toward thy holy oracle.
Draw me not away with the wicked,
  and with the workers of iniquity,
which speak peace to their neighbours,
  but mischief is in their hearts.
Give them according to their deeds,
  and according to the wickedness of their endeavours:
give them after the work of their hands;
  render to them their desert.
Because they regard not the works of the LORD,
  nor the operation of his hands,
he shall destroy them,
  and not build them up.
Blessed be the LORD,
  because he hath heard the voice of my
    supplications.
The LORD is my strength and my shield;
  my heart trusted in him, and I am helped:
therefore my heart greatly rejoiceth;
  and with my song will I praise him.
The LORD is their strength,
  and he is the saving strength of his anointed.
Save thy people, and bless thine inheritance:
  feed them also, and lift them up for ever.

Psalm 28

In you, O Lord, I seek refuge;
  do not let me ever be put to shame;
  in your righteousness deliver me.
Incline your ear to me;
  rescue me speedily.
Be a rock of refuge for me,
  a strong fortress to save me.

You are indeed my rock and my fortress;
  for your name's sake lead me and guide me,
take me out of the net that is hidden for me,

for you are my refuge.
Into your hand I commit my spirit;
   you have redeemed me, O LORD, faithful God…

Be gracious to me, O LORD, for I am in distress;
   my eye wastes away from grief,
   my soul and body also.
For my life is spent with sorrow,
   and my years with sighing;
my strength fails because of my misery,
   and my bones waste away.

I am the scorn of all my adversaries,
   a horror to my neighbours,
an object of dread to my acquaintances;
   those who see me in the street flee from me.
I have passed out of mind like one who is dead;
   I have become like a broken vessel.
For I hear the whispering of many –
   terror all around! –
as they scheme together against me,
   as they plot to take my life.

But I trust in you, O LORD;
   I say, 'You are my God.'
My times are in your hand;
   deliver me from the hand of my enemies and
     persecutors.
Let your face shine upon your servant;
   save me in your steadfast love.
Do not let me be put to shame, O LORD,
   for I call on you;

let the wicked be put to shame;
   let them go dumbfounded to Sheol.
Let the lying lips be stilled
   that speak insolently against the
     righteous
   with pride and contempt...

Blessed be the LORD,
  for he has wondrously shown his steadfast love to me
  when I was beset as a city under siege.
I had said in my alarm,
  'I am driven far from your sight.'
But you heard my supplications
  when I cried out to you for help.

Love the LORD, all you his saints.
  The LORD preserves the faithful,
  but abundantly repays the one who acts haughtily.
Be strong, and let your heart take courage,
  all you who wait for the LORD.

  Psalm 31:1–5, 9–18, 21–24

Save me, O God,
  for the waters have come up to my neck.
I sink in deep mire,
  where there is no foothold;
I have come into deep waters,
  and the flood sweeps over me.
I am weary with my crying;
  my throat is parched.
My eyes grow dim
  with waiting for my God…

But as for me, my prayer is to you, O LORD.
  At an acceptable time, O God,
  in the abundance of your steadfast love, answer me.
With your faithful help rescue me
  from sinking in the mire;

let me be delivered from my enemies
  and from the deep waters.
Do not let the flood sweep over me,
  or the deep swallow me up,
  or the Pit close its mouth over me.

Answer me, O LORD, for your steadfast love is good;
  according to your abundant mercy, turn to me.
Do not hide your face from your servant,
  for I am in distress — make haste to answer me.
Draw near to me, redeem me,
  set me free because of my enemies…

I am lowly and in pain;
　let your salvation, O God, protect me…

Let the oppressed see it and be glad;
　you who seek God, let your hearts revive.
For the LORD hears the needy,
　and does not despise his own that are in bonds.

　　Psalm 69:1–3, 13–18, 29, 32–33

Hear, O LORD, and answer me,
　for I am poor and needy.
Guard my life, for I am devoted to you.
　You are my God; save your servant
　who trusts in you.
Have mercy on me, O Lord,
　for I call to you all day long.
Bring joy to your servant,
　for to you, O Lord,
　I lift up my soul.

You are forgiving and good, O Lord,
　abounding in love to all who call to you.
Hear my prayer, O LORD;
　listen to my cry for mercy.
In the day of my trouble I will call to you,
　for you will answer me.

Among the gods there is none like you, O Lord;
　no deeds can compare with yours.
All the nations you have made
　will come and worship before you, O Lord;

they will bring glory to your name.
For you are great and do marvellous deeds;
   you alone are God...

you, O Lord, are a compassionate and gracious
   God,
   slow to anger, abounding in love and faithfulness.
Turn to me and have mercy on me;
   grant your strength to your servant
   and save the son of your maidservant.
Give me a sign of your goodness,
   that my enemies may see it and be put to shame,
   for you, O LORD, have helped me and comforted me.

    Psalm 86:1–10, 15–17

Bless the LORD, O my soul:
   and all that is within me, bless his holy name.
Bless the LORD, O my soul,
   and forget not all his benefits:
Who forgiveth all thine iniquities;
   who healeth all thy diseases;
Who redeemeth thy life from destruction;
   who crowneth thee with lovingkindness and tender
     mercies;
Who satisfieth thy mouth with good things;
   so that thy youth is renewed like the eagle's.

    Psalm 103:1–5

When You Are Feeling
Guilty

Blessed is he whose transgression is forgiven,
  whose sin is covered.
Blessed is the man unto whom the LORD
      imputeth not iniquity,
  and in whose spirit there is no guile.
When I kept silence, my bones waxed old
  through my roaring all the day long.
For day and night thy hand was heavy
      upon me:
  my moisture is turned into the drought
  of summer.
I acknowledged my sin unto thee,
  and mine iniquity have I not hid.
I said, I will confess my transgressions unto
      the LORD;
  and thou forgavest the iniquity of my sin.
For this shall every one that is godly pray
      unto thee
  in a time when thou mayest be found:
surely in the floods of great waters
  they shall not come nigh unto him.
Thou art my hiding place;
  thou shalt preserve me from trouble;
  thou shalt compass me about with songs
  of deliverance.

  Psalm 32:1–7

O LORD, do not rebuke me in your anger
  or discipline me in your wrath.
For your arrows have pierced me,
  and your hand has come down upon me.

Because of your wrath there is no health in my
  body;
  my bones have no soundness because of my sin.
My guilt has overwhelmed me
  like a burden too heavy to bear.

My wounds fester and are loathsome
  because of my sinful folly.

I am bowed down and brought very low;
   all day long I go about mourning.
My back is filled with searing pain;
   there is no health in my body.
I am feeble and utterly crushed;
   I groan in anguish of heart.

All my longings lie open before you, O Lord;
   my sighing is not hidden from you.
My heart pounds, my strength fails me;
   even the light has gone from my eyes.
My friends and companions avoid me because of
   my wounds;
   my neighbours stay far away.
Those who seek my life set their traps,
   those who would harm me talk of my ruin;
   all day long they plot deception.

I am like a deaf man, who cannot hear,
   like a mute, who cannot open his mouth;
I have become like a man who does not hear,
   whose mouth can offer no reply.
I wait for you, O LORD;
   you will answer, O Lord my God.
For I said, 'Do not let them gloat
   or exalt themselves over me when my foot slips.'

For I am about to fall,
   and my pain is ever with me.
I confess my iniquity;
   I am troubled by my sin.
Many are those who are my vigorous enemies;

those who hate me without reason are
  numerous.
Those who repay my good with evil
  slander me when I pursue what is good.

O LORD, do not forsake me;
  be not far from me, O my God.
Come quickly to help me,
  O Lord my Saviour.

Psalm 38

Have mercy upon me, O God,
   according to thy lovingkindness:
according unto the multitude of thy tender mercies
   blot out my transgressions.
Wash me throughly from mine iniquity,
   and cleanse me from my sin.
For I acknowledge my transgressions:
   and my sin is ever before me.
Against thee, thee only, have I sinned,
   and done this evil in thy sight:
that thou mightest be justified when thou speakest,
   and be clear when thou judgest.
Behold, I was shapen in iniquity;
   and in sin did my mother conceive me.
Behold, thou desirest truth in the inward parts:
   and in the hidden part thou shalt make me to know
    wisdom.
Purge me with hyssop, and I shall be clean:
   wash me, and I shall be whiter than snow.
Make me to hear joy and gladness;
   that the bones which thou hast broken may rejoice.
Hide thy face from my sins,
   and blot out all mine iniquities.
Create in me a clean heart, O God;
   and renew a right spirit within me.
Cast me not away from thy presence;
   and take not thy holy spirit from me.
Restore unto me the joy of thy salvation;
   and uphold me with thy free spirit.
Then will I teach transgressors thy ways;
   and sinners shall be converted unto thee.
Deliver me from bloodguiltiness, O God,

thou God of my salvation:
and my tongue shall sing aloud of thy
    righteousness.
O Lord, open thou my lips;
    and my mouth shall shew forth thy praise.
For thou desirest not sacrifice; else would I give it:
    thou delightest not in burnt offering.
The sacrifices of God are a broken spirit:
    a broken and a contrite heart,

O God, thou wilt not despise.
Do good in thy good pleasure unto Zion:
  build thou the walls of Jerusalem.
Then shalt thou be pleased with the sacrifices of
    righteousness,
  with burnt offering and whole burnt offering:
  then shall they offer bullocks upon thine altar.

    Psalm 51

The LORD is merciful and gracious,
  slow to anger and abounding in steadfast love.
He will not always accuse,
  nor will he keep his anger for ever.
He does not deal with us according to our sins,
  nor repay us according to our iniquities.
For as the heavens are high above the earth,
  so great is his steadfast love towards those who
    fear him;
as far as the east is from the west,
  so far he removes our transgressions from us.
As a father has compassion for his children,
  so the LORD has compassion for those who fear him.
For he knows how we were made;
  he remembers that we are dust.

    Psalm 103:8–14

Out of the depths have I cried unto thee, O LORD.
Lord, hear my voice:
  let thine ears be attentive
  to the voice of my supplications.

If thou, LORD, shouldest mark iniquities,
   O Lord, who shall stand?
But there is forgiveness with thee,
   that thou mayest be feared.
I wait for the LORD, my soul doth wait,
   and in his word do I hope.
My soul waiteth for the Lord
   more than they that watch for the morning:
   I say, more than they that watch for the morning.
Let Israel hope in the LORD:
   for with the LORD there is mercy,
   and with him is plenteous redemption.
And he shall redeem Israel
   from all his iniquities.

Psalm 130

When You Are
Joyful

I will extol thee, O Lord; for thou hast lifted
    me up,
  and hast not made my foes to rejoice over me.
O Lord my God, I cried unto thee,
  and thou hast healed me.
O Lord, thou hast brought up my soul from the
    grave:
  thou hast kept me alive, that I should not go
  down to the pit.
Sing unto the Lord, O ye saints of his,
  and give thanks at the remembrance of his
  holiness.
For his anger endureth but a moment;
  in his favour is life:
weeping may endure for a night,
  but joy cometh in the morning…

Thou hast turned for me my mourning into
    dancing:
  thou hast put off my sackcloth,
  and girded me with gladness;
To the end that my glory may sing praise to thee,
    and not be silent.
  O Lord my God, I will give thanks unto thee
  for ever.

Psalm 30:1–5, 11–12

Sing joyfully to the Lord, you righteous;
  it is fitting for the upright to praise him.
Praise the Lord with the harp;
  make music to him on the ten-stringed lyre.

Sing to him a new song;
  play skilfully, and shout for joy.

For the word of the LORD is right and true;
  he is faithful in all he does.
The LORD loves righteousness and justice;
  the earth is full of his unfailing love.

By the word of the LORD were the heavens made,
  their starry host by the breath of his mouth.
He gathers the waters of the sea into jars;
  he puts the deep into storehouses.
Let all the earth fear the LORD;

let all the people of the world revere him.
For he spoke, and it came to be;
    he commanded, and it stood firm...

We wait in hope for the LORD;
    he is our help and our shield.
In him our hearts rejoice,
    for we trust in his holy name.
May your unfailing love rest upon us, O LORD,
    even as we put our hope in you.

   Psalm 33:1–9, 20–22

O clap your hands, all ye people;
    shout unto God with the voice of triumph.
For the LORD most high is terrible;
    he is a great King over all the earth.
He shall subdue the people under us,
    and the nations under our feet.
He shall choose our inheritance for us,
    the excellency of Jacob whom he loved.
God is gone up with a shout,
    the LORD with the sound of a trumpet.
Sing praises to God, sing praises:
    sing praises unto our King, sing praises.
For God is the King of all the earth:
    sing ye praises with understanding.
God reigneth over the heathen:
    God sitteth upon the throne of his holiness.
The princes of the people are gathered
        together,
    even the people of the God of Abraham:

for the shields of the earth belong unto God:
  he is greatly exalted.

Psalm 47

Make a joyful noise unto God, all ye lands:
Sing forth the honour of his name:
  make his praise glorious.
Say unto God, How terrible art thou in thy works!
  through the greatness of thy power shall thine
    enemies submit themselves unto thee.
All the earth shall worship thee,

and shall sing unto thee;
  they shall sing to thy name.
Come and see the works of God:
  he is terrible in his doing toward the children
    of men.
He turned the sea into dry land:
  they went through the flood on foot:
  there did we rejoice in him.
He ruleth by his power for ever;
  his eyes behold the nations:
  let not the rebellious exalt themselves.

O bless our God, ye people,
   and make the voice of his praise to be heard:
Which holdeth our soul in life,
   and suffereth not our feet to be moved.
For thou, O God, hast proved us:
   thou hast tried us, as silver is tried.
Thou broughtest us into the net;
   thou laidst affliction upon our loins.
Thou hast caused men to ride over our heads;
   we went through fire and through water:
but thou broughtest us out into a wealthy place.

I will go into thy house with burnt offerings:
  I will pay thee my vows,
Which my lips have uttered, and my mouth hath spoken,
  when I was in trouble.
I will offer unto thee burnt sacrifices of fatlings,
  with the incense of rams;
I will offer bullocks with goats.
Come and hear, all ye that fear God,
  and I will declare what he hath done for my soul.
I cried unto him with my mouth,
  and he was extolled with my tongue.
If I regard iniquity in my heart,
  the Lord will not hear me:
But verily God hath heard me;
  he hath attended to the voice of my prayer.
Blessed be God,
  which hath not turned away my prayer,
  nor his mercy from me.

  Psalm 66

The LORD reigneth; let the earth rejoice;
  let the multitude of isles be glad thereof.
Clouds and darkness are round about him:
  righteousness and judgment are the habitation of
    his throne.
A fire goeth before him,
  and burneth up his enemies round about.
His lightnings enlightened the world:
  the earth saw, and trembled.
The hills melted like wax at the presence of the LORD,
  at the presence of the Lord of the whole earth.

The heavens declare his righteousness,
  and all the people see his glory.
Confounded be all they that serve graven images,
  that boast themselves of idols:
  worship him, all ye gods.
Zion heard, and was glad;
  and the daughters of Judah rejoiced
  because of thy judgments, O LORD.
For thou, LORD, art high above all the earth:
  thou art exalted far above all gods.
Ye that love the LORD, hate evil:
  he preserveth the souls of his saints;
  he delivereth them out of the hand of the wicked.
Light is sown for the righteous,
  and gladness for the upright in heart.

Rejoice in the LORD, ye righteous;
and give thanks at the remembrance of his holiness.

Psalm 97

Praise ye the LORD.
Sing unto the LORD a new song,
and his praise in the congregation of saints.
Let Israel rejoice in him that made him:
let the children of Zion be joyful in their King.
Let them praise his name in the dance:
let them sing praises unto him with the timbrel
and harp.
For the LORD taketh pleasure in his people:
he will beautify the meek with salvation.
Let the saints be joyful in glory:
let them sing aloud upon their beds.
Let the high praises of God be in their mouth,
and a twoedged sword in their hand;
To execute vengeance upon the heathen,
and punishments upon the people;
To bind their kings with chains,
and their nobles with fetters of iron;
To execute upon them the judgment written:
this honour have all his saints.
Praise ye the LORD.

Psalm 149

When You Are
Lonely

Give ear to my words, O Lord,
  consider my meditation.
Hearken unto the voice of my cry,
  my King, and my God:
  for unto thee will I pray.
My voice shalt thou hear in the morning, O Lord;
  in the morning will I direct my prayer unto thee,
  and will look up.
For thou art not a God that hath pleasure in
    wickedness:
  neither shall evil dwell with thee.
The foolish shall not stand in thy sight:
  thou hatest all workers of iniquity.
Thou shalt destroy them that speak leasing
    [falsehood]:
  the Lord will abhor the bloody and deceitful man.
But as for me, I will come into thy house
  in the multitude of thy mercy:
and in thy fear will I worship
  toward thy holy temple.
Lead me, O Lord, in thy righteousness
  because of mine enemies;
  make thy way straight before my face.
For there is no faithfulness in their mouth;
  their inward part is very wickedness;
their throat is an open sepulchre;
  they flatter with their tongue.
Destroy thou them, O God;
  let them fall by their own counsels;
cast them out in the multitude of their
    transgressions;
  for they have rebelled against thee.

But let all those that put their trust in thee rejoice:
    let them ever shout for joy,
because thou defendest them:
    let them also that love thy name be joyful in thee.
For thou, LORD, wilt bless the righteous;
    with favour wilt thou compass him as with a shield.

Psalm 5

To you, O LORD, I lift up my soul.
O my God, in you I trust;
    do not let me be put to shame;
    do not let my enemies exult over me.
Do not let those who wait for you be put to shame;
    let them be ashamed who are wantonly
        treacherous…

Be mindful of your mercy, O LORD, and of your
    steadfast love,
  for they have been from of old.
Do not remember the sins of my youth or my
    transgressions;
    according to your steadfast love remember me,
    for your goodness' sake, O LORD!...

The friendship of the LORD is for those who
    fear him,
  and he makes his covenant known to them.
My eyes are ever towards the LORD,
  for he will pluck my feet out of the net.

Turn to me and be gracious to me,
  for I am lonely and afflicted.
Relieve the troubles of my heart,
  and bring me out of my distress.
Consider my affliction and my trouble,
  and forgive all my sins.

Consider how many are my foes,
  and with what violent hatred they hate me.
O guard my life, and deliver me;
  do not let me be put to shame, for I take refuge
    in you.
May integrity and uprightness preserve me,
  for I wait for you.

Redeem Israel, O God,
  out of all its troubles.

Psalm 25:1–3, 6–7, 14–22

Hear my prayer, O LORD;
  let my cry come to you.
Do not hide your face from me
  in the day of my distress.
Incline your ear to me;
   answer me speedily on the day when I call...

I am like an owl of the wilderness,
  like a little owl of the waste places.
I lie awake;
  I am like a lonely bird on the housetop.
All day long my enemies taunt me;
   those who deride me use my name for a curse...

My days are like an evening shadow;
  I wither away like grass.

But you, O LORD, are enthroned for ever;
  your name endures to all generations.
You will rise up and have compassion on Zion,
  for it is time to favour it;
  the appointed time has come...

For the LORD will build up Zion;
  he will appear in his glory.
He will regard the prayer of the destitute,
  and will not despise their prayer.

    Psalm 102:1–2, 6–8, 11–13, 16–17

O LORD, thou hast searched me, and known me.
Thou knowest my downsitting and mine uprising,

thou understandest my thought afar off.
Thou compassest my path and my lying down,
  and art acquainted with all my ways.
For there is not a word in my tongue,
  but, lo, O LORD, thou knowest it altogether.
Thou hast beset me behind and before,
  and laid thine hand upon me.
Such knowledge is too wonderful for me;
  it is high, I cannot attain unto it.
Whither shall I go from thy spirit?
  or whither shall I flee from thy presence?
If I ascend up into heaven, thou art there:
  if I make my bed in hell, behold, thou art there.
If I take the wings of the morning,
  and dwell in the uttermost parts of the sea;
Even there shall thy hand lead me,
  and thy right hand shall hold me.
If I say, Surely the darkness shall cover me;
  even the night shall be light about me.
Yea, the darkness hideth not from thee;
  but the night shineth as the day:
  the darkness and the light are both alike to thee.
For thou hast possessed my reins:
  thou hast covered me in my mother's womb.
I will praise thee; for I am fearfully and wonderfully
  made:
  marvellous are thy works;
  and that my soul knoweth right well.
My substance was not hid from thee,
  when I was made in secret,
  and curiously wrought in the lowest parts of the
  earth.

Thine eyes did see my substance, yet being unperfect;
and in thy book all my members were written,
  which in continuance were fashioned,
  when as yet there was none of them.
How precious also are thy thoughts unto me,
   O God!
  how great is the sum of them!
If I should count them, they are more in number
   than the sand:
  when I awake,
  I am still with thee...

Search me, O God, and know my heart:
  try me, and know my thoughts:
And see if there be any wicked way in me,
  and lead me in the way everlasting.

Psalm 139:1–18, 23–24

I cry aloud to the LORD;
  I lift up my voice to the LORD for mercy.
I pour out my complaint before him;
  before him I tell my trouble.

When my spirit grows faint within me,
  it is you who know my way.
In the path where I walk
  men have hidden a snare for me.
Look to my right and see;
  no one is concerned for me.
I have no refuge;
  no one cares for my life.

I cry to you, O LORD;
  I say, 'You are my refuge,
  my portion in the land of the living.'
Listen to my cry,
  for I am in desperate need;
rescue me from those who pursue me,
  for they are too strong for me.
Set me free from my prison,
  that I may praise your name.

Then the righteous will gather about me
  because of your goodness to me.

Psalm 142

When You Are
Needing Guidance

Blessed is the man
who does not walk in the counsel of the wicked
or stand in the way of sinners
or sit in the seat of mockers.
But his delight is in the law of the LORD,
and on his law he meditates day and night.
He is like a tree planted by streams of water,
which yields its fruit in season
and whose leaf does not wither.
Whatever he does prospers.

Not so the wicked!
They are like chaff
that the wind blows away.
Therefore the wicked will not stand in the judgment,
nor sinners in the assembly of the righteous.

For the LORD watches over the way of the righteous,
but the way of the wicked will perish.

Psalm 1

The law of the LORD is perfect,
converting the soul:
the testimony of the LORD is sure,
making wise the simple.
The statutes of the LORD are right,
rejoicing the heart:
the commandment of the LORD is pure,
enlightening the eyes.
The fear of the LORD is clean,
enduring for ever:

the judgments of the LORD are true
  and righteous altogether.
More to be desired are they than gold,
  yea, than much fine gold:
sweeter also than honey
  and the honeycomb.
Moreover by them is thy servant warned:
  and in keeping of them there is great reward.
Who can understand his errors?
  cleanse thou me from secret faults.
Keep back thy servant also from presumptuous
    sins;
  let them not have dominion over me:
then shall I be upright,
  and I shall be innocent from the great
    transgression.
Let the words of my mouth, and the meditation of
    my heart,
  be acceptable in thy sight,
  O LORD, my strength, and my redeemer.

  Psalm 19:7–14

Make me to know your ways, O LORD;
  teach me your paths.
Lead me in your truth, and teach me,
  for you are the God of my salvation;
  for you I wait all day long…

Good and upright is the LORD;
  therefore he instructs sinners in the way.
He leads the humble in what is right,

and teaches the humble his way.
All the paths of the LORD are steadfast love and
 faithfulness,
 for those who keep his covenant and his decrees.

For your name's sake, O LORD,
 pardon my guilt, for it is great.
Who are they that fear the LORD?
 He will teach them the way that they should
 choose.

Psalm 25:4–5, 8–12

I will instruct you and teach you the way you
    should go;
  I will counsel you with my eye upon you.
Do not be like a horse or a mule, without
    understanding,
  whose temper must be curbed with bit and
    bridle,
  else it will not stay near you.

Many are the torments of the wicked,
  but steadfast love surrounds those who trust in
    the LORD.
Be glad in the LORD and rejoice, O righteous,
  and shout for joy, all you upright in heart.

  Psalm 32:8–11

Trust in the LORD, and do good;
  so shalt thou dwell in the land, and verily thou
    shalt be fed.
Delight thyself also in the LORD;
  and he shall give thee the desires of thine heart.
Commit thy way unto the LORD;
  trust also in him; and he shall bring it to pass.
And he shall bring forth thy righteousness as the
    light,
  and thy judgment as the noonday.
Rest in the LORD, and wait patiently for him:
  fret not thyself because of him who prospereth in
    his way,
  because of the man who bringeth wicked devices
    to pass…

The steps of a good man are ordered by
   the LORD:
  and he delighteth in his way.
Though he fall, he shall not be utterly cast down:
  for the LORD upholdeth him with his hand.
I have been young, and now am old;
  yet have I not seen the righteous forsaken,
  nor his seed begging bread.
He is ever merciful, and lendeth;
  and his seed is blessed...

Wait on the LORD, and keep his way,
  and he shall exalt thee to inherit the land:
  when the wicked are cut off, thou shalt see it...

the salvation of the righteous is of the LORD:
  he is their strength in the time of trouble.
And the LORD shall help them, and deliver them:
  he shall deliver them from the wicked, and save
    them,
  because they trust in him.

    Psalm 37:3–7, 23–26, 34, 39–40

Teach me your way, O LORD,
  and I will walk in your truth;
give me an undivided heart,
  that I may fear your name.
I will praise you, O Lord my God, with all my heart;
  I will glorify your name for ever.
For great is your love towards me;
  you have delivered me from the depths of the grave.

    Psalm 86:11–13

How can a young man keep his way pure?
  By living according to your word.
I seek you with all my heart;
  do not let me stray from your commands.
I have hidden your word in my heart
  that I might not sin against you.
Praise be to you, O LORD;
  teach me your decrees.
With my lips I recount
  all the laws that come from your mouth.
I rejoice in following your statutes
  as one rejoices in great riches.

I meditate on your precepts
  and consider your ways.
I delight in your decrees;
  I will not neglect your word…

Your word is a lamp to my feet
  and a light for my path.
I have taken an oath and confirmed it,
  that I will follow your righteous laws.
I have suffered much;
  preserve my life, O LORD, according to your word.
Accept, O LORD, the willing praise of my mouth,

and teach me your laws.
Though I constantly take my life in my hands,
   I will not forget your law.
The wicked have set a snare for me,
   but I have not strayed from your precepts.
Your statutes are my heritage for ever;
   they are the joy of my heart.
My heart is set on keeping your decrees
   to the very end.

Psalm 119:9–16, 105–112

When You Are
Discouraged

Protect me, O God, for in you I take refuge.
I say to the LORD, 'You are my Lord;
  I have no good apart from you.'

As for the holy ones in the land, they are the noble,
  in whom is all my delight.

Those who choose another god multiply their sorrows;
  their drink offerings of blood I will not pour out
  or take their names upon my lips…

I bless the LORD who gives me counsel;
  in the night also my heart instructs me.
I keep the LORD always before me;
  because he is at my right hand, I shall not be moved.

Therefore my heart is glad, and my soul rejoices;
  my body also rests secure.
For you do not give me up to Sheol,
  or let your faithful one see the Pit.

You show me the path of life.
  In your presence there is fullness of joy;
  in your right hand are pleasures for evermore.

  Psalm 16:1–4, 7–11

I waited patiently for the LORD;
  and he inclined unto me, and heard my cry.
He brought me up also out of an horrible pit,
  out of the miry clay,
and set my feet upon a rock,

and established my goings.
And he hath put a new song in my mouth,
   even praise unto our God:
many shall see it, and fear,
   and shall trust in the LORD.
Blessed is that man
   that maketh the LORD his trust,
and respecteth not the proud,
   nor such as turn aside to lies.
Many, O LORD my God,
   are thy wonderful works which thou hast done,
      and thy thoughts which are to us-ward:
   they cannot be reckoned up in order unto thee:
if I would declare and speak of them,
   they are more than can be numbered.
Sacrifice and offering thou didst not desire;
   mine ears hast thou opened:
burnt offering and sin offering
   hast thou not required.
Then said I, Lo, I come:
   in the volume of the book it is written of me,
I delight to do thy will, O my God:
   yea, thy law is within my heart...

Withhold not thou
   thy tender mercies from me, O LORD:
let thy lovingkindness and thy truth
   continually preserve me.
For innumerable evils
   have compassed me about:
mine iniquities have taken hold upon me,
   so that I am not able to look up;

they are more than the hairs of mine head:
  therefore my heart faileth me.
Be pleased, O LORD, to deliver me:
  O LORD, make haste to help me.
Let them be ashamed and confounded together
  that seek after my soul to destroy it;
let them be driven backward and put to shame
  that wish me evil.
Let them be desolate for a reward of their shame
  that say unto me, Aha, aha.
Let all those that seek thee
  rejoice and be glad in thee:
let such as love thy salvation say continually,
  The LORD be magnified.
But I am poor and needy;

yet the Lord thinketh upon me:
thou art my help and my deliverer;
  make no tarrying, O my God.

    Psalm 40:1–8, 11–17

As the hart panteth after the water brooks,
  so panteth my soul after thee, O God.
My soul thirsteth for God, for the living God:
  when shall I come and appear before God?
My tears have been my meat
  day and night,
while they continually say unto me,
  Where is thy God?
When I remember these things,
  I pour out my soul in me:
for I had gone with the multitude,
  I went with them to the house of God,
with the voice of joy and praise,
  with a multitude that kept holyday.
Why art thou cast down, O my soul?
  and why art thou disquieted in me?
hope thou in God: for I shall yet praise him
  for the help of his countenance.
O my God, my soul is cast down within me:
  therefore will I remember thee
from the land of Jordan, and of the Hermonites,
  from the hill Mizar.
Deep calleth unto deep
  at the noise of thy waterspouts:
all thy waves and thy billows
  are gone over me.

Yet the LORD will command his lovingkindness
   in the daytime,
  and in the night his song shall be with me,
  and my prayer unto the God of my life.
I will say unto God my rock,
  Why hast thou forgotten me?
why go I mourning
  because of the oppression of the enemy?
As with a sword in my bones,
  mine enemies reproach me;
while they say daily unto me,
  Where is thy God?
Why art thou cast down, O my soul?
  and why art thou disquieted within me?
hope thou in God: for I shall yet praise him,
  who is the health of my countenance, and my God.

Psalm 42

Give ear to my prayer, O God;
  and hide not thyself from my supplication.
Attend unto me, and hear me:
  I mourn in my complaint, and make a noise;
Because of the voice of the enemy,
  because of the oppression of the wicked:
for they cast iniquity upon me,
  and in wrath they hate me.
My heart is sore pained within me:
  and the terrors of death are fallen upon me.
Fearfulness and trembling are come upon me,
  and horror hath overwhelmed me.
And I said, Oh that I had wings like a dove!

for then would I fly away, and be at rest.
Lo, then would I wander far off,
    and remain in the wilderness.
I would hasten my escape
    from the windy storm and tempest...

As for me, I will call upon God;
    and the LORD shall save me.
Evening, and morning, and at noon,
    will I pray, and cry aloud:
    and he shall hear my voice.
He hath delivered my soul in peace
    from the battle that was against me:
    for there were many with me...

Cast thy burden upon the LORD,
  and he shall sustain thee:
he shall never suffer
  the righteous to be moved.

    Psalm 55:1–8, 16–18, 22

I will lift up mine eyes unto the hills,
  from whence cometh my help.
My help cometh from the LORD,
  which made heaven and earth.
He will not suffer thy foot to be moved:
  he that keepeth thee will not slumber.
Behold, he that keepeth Israel
  shall neither slumber nor sleep.
The LORD is thy keeper:
  the LORD is thy shade upon thy right hand.
The sun shall not smite thee by day,
  nor the moon by night.
The LORD shall preserve thee from all evil:
  he shall preserve thy soul.
The LORD shall preserve thy going out and thy
    coming in
  from this time forth, and even for evermore.

    Psalm 121

When You Are
Worshipful

O Lord our Lord,
how excellent is thy name in all the earth!
who hast set thy glory above the heavens.
Out of the mouth of babes and sucklings
hast thou ordained strength because of
thine enemies,
that thou mightest still the enemy and the avenger.
When I consider thy heavens, the work of
thy fingers,
the moon and the stars, which thou hast ordained;
What is man, that thou art mindful of him?
and the son of man, that thou visitest him?
For thou hast made him a little lower than
the angels,
and hast crowned him with glory and honour.
Thou madest him to have dominion over the works
of thy hands;
thou hast put all things under his feet:
All sheep and oxen,
yea, and the beasts of the field;
The fowl of the air, and the fish of the sea,
and whatsoever passeth through the paths of
the seas.
O Lord our Lord,
how excellent is thy name in all the earth!

Psalm 8

O come, let us sing unto the Lord:
let us make a joyful noise to the rock of our
salvation.
Let us come before his presence with thanksgiving,

and make a joyful noise unto him with psalms.
For the LORD is a great God,
    and a great King above all gods.
In his hand are the deep places of the earth:
    the strength of the hills is his also.
The sea is his, and he made it:
    and his hands formed the dry land.
O come, let us worship and bow down:
    let us kneel before the LORD our maker.
For he is our God;
    and we are the people of his pasture,
    and the sheep of his hand.
To day if ye will hear his voice,
    Harden not your heart, as in the provocation,
    and as in the day of temptation in the wilderness:
When your fathers tempted me,
    proved me, and saw my work.
Forty years long was I grieved with this generation,
    and said, It is a people that do err in their heart,
    and they have not known my ways:
Unto whom I sware in my wrath
    that they should not enter into my rest.

Psalm 95

O sing unto the LORD a new song:
    sing unto the LORD, all the earth.
Sing unto the LORD, bless his name;
    shew forth his salvation from day to day.
Declare his glory among the heathen,
    his wonders among all people.
For the LORD is great, and greatly to be praised:

he is to be feared above all gods.
For all the gods of the nations are idols:
  but the LORD made the heavens.
Honour and majesty are before him:
  strength and beauty are in his sanctuary.
Give unto the LORD, O ye kindreds of the people,
  give unto the LORD glory and strength.
Give unto the LORD the glory due unto his name:
  bring an offering, and come into his courts.
O worship the LORD in the beauty of holiness:
  fear before him, all the earth.

Say among the heathen that the LORD reigneth:
  the world also shall be established that it shall not
    be moved:
  he shall judge the people righteously.
Let the heavens rejoice, and let the earth be glad;
  let the sea roar, and the fullness thereof.
Let the field be joyful, and all that is therein:
  then shall all the trees of the wood rejoice
Before the LORD: for he cometh,
  for he cometh to judge the earth:
he shall judge the world with righteousness,
  and the people with his truth.

Psalm 96

Make a joyful noise unto the LORD, all ye lands.
Serve the LORD with gladness:
  come before his presence with singing.
Know ye that the LORD he is God:
  it is he that hath made us, and not we ourselves;
  we are his people, and the sheep of his pasture.
Enter into his gates with thanksgiving,
  and into his courts with praise:
  be thankful unto him, and bless his name.
For the LORD is good;
  his mercy is everlasting;
  and his truth endureth to all generations.

Psalm 100

Praise ye the LORD.
I will praise the LORD with my whole heart,

in the assembly of the upright, and in the
   congregation.
The works of the LORD are great,
   sought out of all them that have pleasure therein.
His work is honourable and glorious:
   and his righteousness endureth for ever.
He hath made his wonderful works to be
      remembered:
   the LORD is gracious and full of compassion.
He hath given meat unto them that fear him:
   he will ever be mindful of his covenant.
He hath shewed his people the power of his works,
   that he may give them the heritage of the heathen.
The works of his hands are verity and judgment;
   all his commandments are sure.
They stand fast for ever and ever,
   and are done in truth and uprightness.
He sent redemption unto his people:
   he hath commanded his covenant for ever:
   holy and reverend is his name.
The fear of the LORD is the beginning of wisdom:
   a good understanding have all they that do his
      commandments:
   his praise endureth for ever.

   Psalm 111

I will extol thee, my God, O king;
   and I will bless thy name for ever and ever.
Every day will I bless thee;
   and I will praise thy name for ever and ever.
Great is the LORD, and greatly to be praised;

and his greatness is unsearchable.
One generation shall praise thy works to another,
    and shall declare thy mighty acts.
I will speak of the glorious honour of thy majesty,
    and of thy wondrous works.
And men shall speak of the might of thy terrible acts:
    and I will declare thy greatness.
They shall abundantly utter the memory of thy great
        goodness,
    and shall sing of thy righteousness.
The Lord is gracious, and full of compassion;
    slow to anger, and of great mercy.
The Lord is good to all:
    and his tender mercies are over all his works.

All thy works shall praise thee, O LORD;
  and thy saints shall bless thee.
They shall speak of the glory of thy kingdom,
  and talk of thy power;
To make known to the sons of men his mighty acts,
  and the glorious majesty of his kingdom.
Thy kingdom is an everlasting kingdom,
  and thy dominion endureth throughout all
    generations.
The LORD upholdeth all that fall,
  and raiseth up all those that be bowed down.
The eyes of all wait upon thee;
  and thou givest them their meat in due season.
Thou openest thine hand,
  and satisfiest the desire of every living thing.
The LORD is righteous in all his ways,
  and holy in all his works.
The LORD is nigh unto all them that call upon him,
  to all that call upon him in truth.
He will fulfil the desire of them that fear him:
  he also will hear their cry, and will save them.
The LORD preserveth all them that love him:
  but all the wicked will he destroy.
My mouth shall speak the praise of the LORD:
  and let all flesh bless his holy name for ever
    and ever.

Psalm 145

Praise ye the LORD.
Praise God in his sanctuary:
  praise him in the firmament of his power.